John W. Sch
MAKING MUSIC at the PIANO

T0085075

LEVEL SEVEN

(Formerly Book 8)

FOREWORD

This improved edition incorporates numerous refinements, compiled by a team of piano teaching experts, which are based on the evaluation of extensive use in actual teaching situations during the past 15 years. The result is a volume that combines the proven merit and usefulness of the original edition with added benefits for students and ease of use for teachers.

Level Seven places emphasis on unique repertoire selections, many of which are suitable for contest or audition use. Music appreciation information about the source of the music and each composer is an important part of this book. It features an original sonata with a detailed outline and analysis of the form, plus an original two-part fugue with an explanation.

Technical progress is made through interlocking chromatic passages, alternating hands, left-hand velocity, extended arpeggios, plus numerous other etudes. 5/4 time, the double-dot, key of G-flat major, and the cadenza are introduced. *Self-help* is encouraged by the Reference Pages (front and back inside covers) and the Music Dictionary (page 48), which is customized for this book.

PROGRESSIVE SUCCESSION of MAKING MUSIC at the PIANO

Primer Level (Preparatory)
Includes the *Schaum Keyboard Touch Finder,* a teaching aid that helps establish good sight-reading habits from the first lesson: keeping eyes on the music.

Level One (A or Grade 1)
Develops transposition; encourages creativeness. Explores 4 new keys, staccato, chords, and cross-hands.

Level Two (B or Grade 1½)
Special emphasis on rhythm patterns and forms. Music appreciation stories, pictures, and facts.

Level Three (C or Grade 2)
Triads and broken chords in many keys. Accents, trills, triplets, grace notes, dotted 8th notes, 9/8 time, etc.

Level Four (D or Grade 2½)
Minor scales and pieces, polyphonic music, finger velocity, and an extensive variety of music styles.

Level Five (E or Grade 3)
Arpeggios, embellishments, chromatic and whole-tone scales, etc. Impressionistic and modern selections.

Level Six (F or Grade 4)
Hand expansion, octave technic, 2-against-3, rubato, 16th note triplet, double flat, glissando, pedal point.

Level Seven (G-H or Grade 4½-5)
Sonata, fugue, 5/4 time, cadenza, extended arpeggios, tenth bass, quintuplets, interlocking octave technic.

SCHAUM PUBLICATIONS, INC.

10235 N. Port Washington Rd.   Mequon, WI 53092

CONTENTS

TO THE TEACHER

Student musicianship is developed by a well-balanced curriculum that teaches note reading, finger strength and dexterity, music theory, and music appreciation. It is recommended that one *theory* book, one *technic* book, and several *repertoire* selections be used to supplement this book.

Review work and memorization should be a regular part of the student's assignments. As the pupil advances through the book, there will be pieces that are especially well-liked. These are good choices for memory work. An accumulation of memorized pieces becomes the student's repertoire. The *Music Dictionary* on page 48 is designed for self-help.

LEVEL SEVEN Teaching Program
REPERTOIRE Books:
Sacred Music:
GOSPEL CAMEOS
GOSPEL PIANO PROFILES

SPIRITUAL CAMEOS

Original Classics:
AMERICAN COMPOSERS
of the 20th CENTURY
BACH: TWO-PART INVENTIONS
COMPOSER-PIANISTS
CONTEMPORARY COMPOSERS

Casual Style:
BOOGIE ARTISTRY
PRESTIGE PIANO SOLOS

Sheet Music Solos:
After Theater Tango *(Zez Confrey)*
Humoresque *(Dvorak)*

Mexican Hat Dance *(Transcription)*
Symphonic Rhapsody *(Cesar Franck)*

Garden of Dreams
(Mattinata)

Ruggero Leoncavallo (roog-YAIR-oh lay-on-cah-VAL-loh), an Italian composer and librettist born in Naples, studied music at the Naples Conservatory and literature at Bologna University. He is known only for the famous opera, "Pagliacci," (meaning *The Clowns*). This piece is transcribed from that opera.

R. Leoncavallo (1858-1919)

Torch Dance

Edward German was an English composer whose real name was Edward German Jones. He began the study of piano and organ at age five. He taught himself to play the violin and later studied at the Royal Academy of Music in London where he achieved many honors. This piece is transcribed from a suite for orchestra which he wrote for Shakespeare's play, "Henry VIII."

Edward German
(1862–1936)

Note: The performance of the broken tenth bass is illustrated below. The accented note is struck precisely on the beat.

As written   As played

Madame Butterfly

Giacomo Puccini (jee-AH-koe-moe poo-CHEE-nee) was a famous Italian opera composer. He was trained to take over his father's position as town organist and choirmaster. However, he was so strongly influenced by the operas of Giuseppe Verdi that he turned instead to composing. "La Boheme," "Tosca," and "Madame Butterfly" are Puccini's most famous operas. This piece is transcribed from his opera, "Madame Butterfly," the tragic story of a Japanese woman married to an American navy officer.

G. Puccini (1858-1924)

Fury
(Arabeske)

Allegro M.M. ♩ = 112

Stephen Heller * (1813-1888)

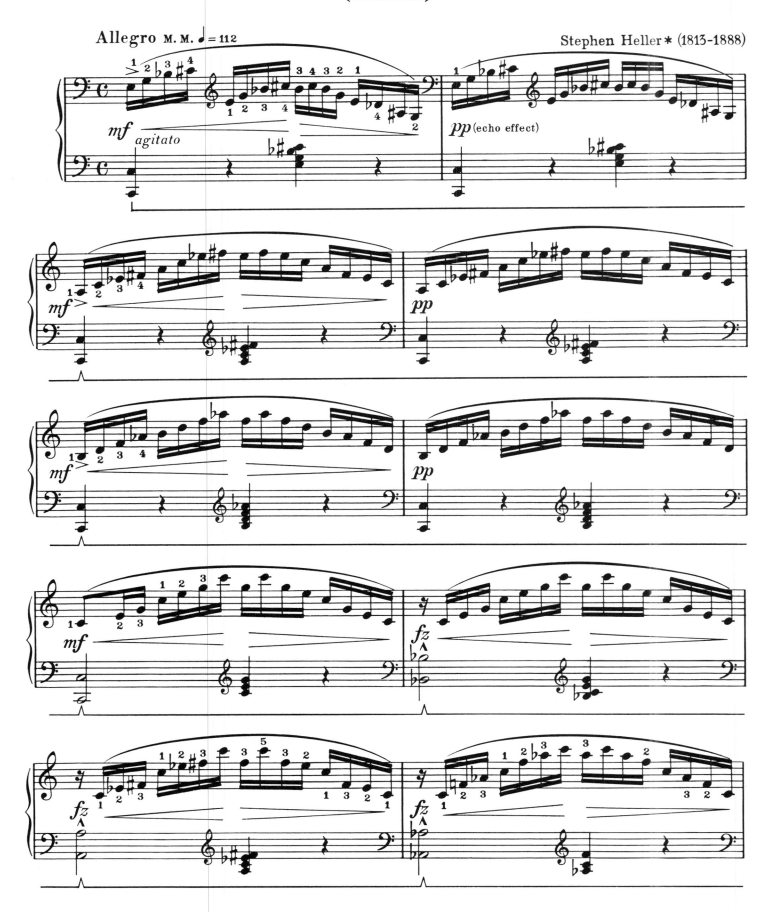

* Stephen Heller was a Hungarian composer and pianist. Through his teacher, Anton Halm, Heller was introduced to Schubert and Beethoven. Heller gave concerts in Hungary, Transylvania, Poland, and Germany. His music was admired by the French composers, Bizet and Massenet. Heller received the French Legion d'honneur in recognition of his accomplishments.

Procession of the Pachyderms

(Marche Fantastique)

Wilson G. Smith, Op. 73

Pachyderm is a flamboyant name applied to elephants by circus people. The music is appropriately heavy and ponderous. Wilson G. Smith (1859-1929) was an American composer who studied in Berlin, Germany and afterwards worked as a piano teacher and composer in Cleveland, Ohio.

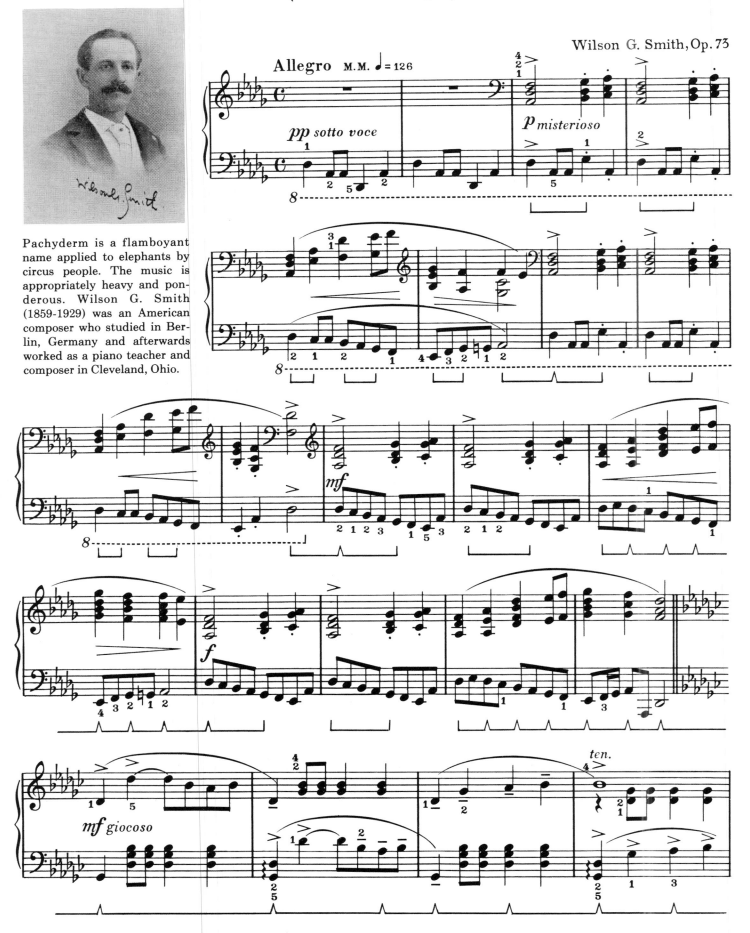

Sailors' Dance

Reinhold Gliere (glee-AIR) was honored many times by the Russian government for his ballets, operas, symphonies, and concertos. He taught at the Moscow Conservatory and is considered the founder of Soviet Ballet. This piece is transcribed from his ballet, "The Red Poppy."

A *cadenza* (kah-DEN-zah) appears at the bottom of page 16. It is an elaborate ornamental musical passage exhibiting the skills of a solo performer.

Reinhold Gliere (1875-1956)

Take Five

Edward Poldini (poll-DEE-nee), 1869-1957, was a Hungarian composer whose operettas and piano compositions were known throughout most of Europe. He was awarded honors for his music by the Hungarian government. This piece is condensed from one of his piano compositions originally titled, "Humoresque" (see music dictionary on page 48).

When playing 5/4 time, it is helpful to think of each measure as being groups of 2 + 3 counts, as illustrated here. For accurate rhythm, use a metronome to be sure that all five counts are equally spaced.

Flotsam and Jetsam

(Two-part Fugue)

A fugue is a musical creation formed from a single melody. First the theme is announced in one voice alone, then it is enunciated in due succession in other voices weaving progressively into a complex tapestry of themes. That portion of a fugue in which the theme is asserted at least once in each voice is called an EXPOSITION. Fugues usually consist of three or more expositions.

Flotsam and Jetsam are nautical terms. Flotsam refers to bits of wreckage of a ship found *floating* on the surface of the sea. Jetsam applies to articles *below* the surface of the water such as cargo cast overboard to lighten a vessel in danger of being ship-wrecked. Appropriately in the following fugue, the lower voice represents *jetsam* and the upper voice portrays *flotsam*.

John W. Schaum

Old Curiosity Shop

Selim Palmgren was born in Finland and is best known for his short piano pieces. After giving a concert tour in the United States, he joined the faculty of the Eastman School of Music in Rochester, New York. He later returned to Helsinki, Finland where he was a professor at the Sibelius Academy of Music. This piece, appearing here in its original form, was first titled, "Rococo."

Selim Palmgren (1878-1951)

Note: The manner of playing the broken chord in the right hand is illustrated below. The notes are played in rapid succession from the bottom up. All the tones are held down and the top note is accented.

As written: As played:

Follow the above procedure whenever a broken chord occurs.

* Chords indicated with an asterisk need the bottom note (middle-C) released early to allow the left hand to play the same note. The upper notes of these chords are to be held for their full value. (Page 20, line 2, measure 3; and page 21, line 5, measure 2.)

Fox and Hounds

Joseph Rheinberger ∗ (1839–1901)

* Joseph Rheinberger (RINE-ber-ger) was a German composer, conductor, organist, pianist, and teacher. He started organ lessons at age 5 and was a church organist at age 7! His sonatas for organ are probably his best known compositions. This piece is condensed from an original piano solo which was titled, "The Chase."

Paris Nocturne

Maurice Ravel (rah-VELL) was one of France's greatest composers, famous for his piano solos and orchestral music, especially ballets. He was one of the best known composers using impressionistic style (see Dictionary on page 48) and experimented with many unusual harmonies and effects at the keyboard. This piece is transcribed from his piano solo, "Sonatine."

Maurice Ravel (1875–1937)

The Moldau River

Bedrich Smetana (SMET-tah-nah), 1824-1884, was Bohemia's most famous composer whose music reflected its legends, history and scenery. (Bohemia is now part of Czechoslovakia.) Smetana is best known for his operas and symphonic poems. This piece is transcribed from a symphonic poem titled, "The Moldau," which is a river in Bohemia. The accompaniment represents the movement of the river waters.

B. Smetana

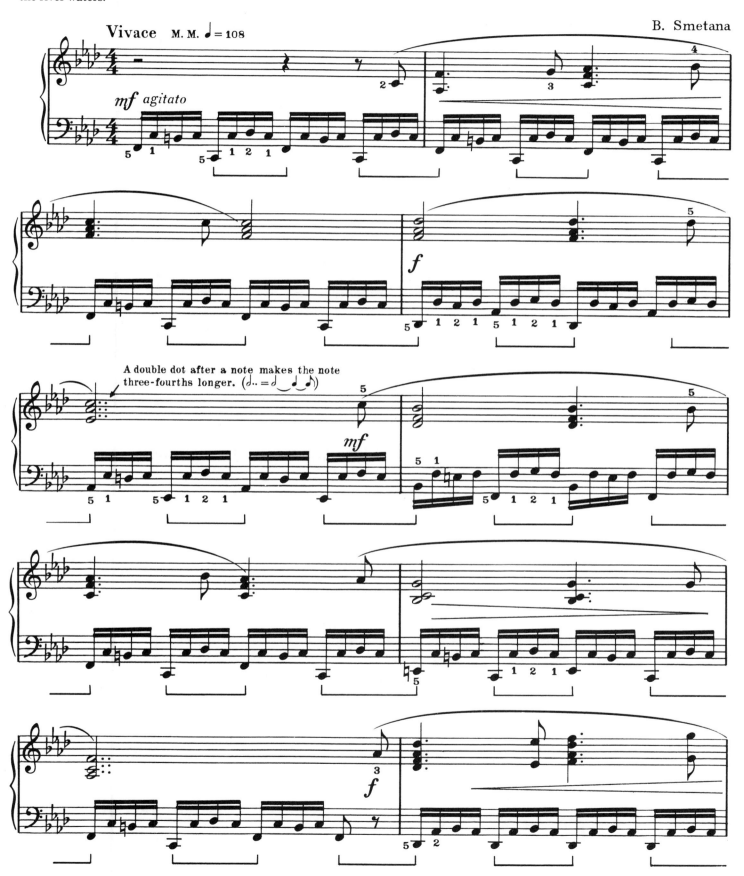

Sheet Music suggestion: **MEXICAN HAT DANCE** *(Concert Transcription)*

SEA ROVER SONATA

(Analysis of the Sonata Form)

A sonata is a large extended composition for solo instrument consisting of a series of movements (usually three or four) which vary in rhythm and mood but are related in tonality and which have a basic unity of feeling and design. A symphony is an orchestral piece written in the sonata form.

The "Sea Rover Sonata" is composed in the authentic form and style of the traditional classical sonata. Songs and dances of the sea provide the thematic material on which the sonata is built.

FIRST MOVEMENT

"Bell Bottom Trousers" and "Strike Up the Band, Here Comes a Sailor"

The first movement is separated into the following subdivisions:

EXPOSITION . . . . . Principal Theme ("Bell Bottom Trousers" in D major).
Transition (To the dominant key).
Subordinate Theme ("Strike Up the Band, Here Comes a Sailor" in A major).
Closing Theme (A major).

DEVELOPMENT . . . . This section is an improvisation based on themes selected from the *Exposition*.

RECAPITULATION . . . Principal Theme ("Bell Bottom Trousers" in D major).
Transition (To the tonic key).
Subordinate Theme ("Strike Up the Band, Here Comes a Sailor" in D major).
Closing Theme (Various keys).
Coda (Ending pattern).

SECOND MOVEMENT

"Rocked in the Cradle of the Deep"

This legendary nautical hymn is a prayer for the safety of all seafaring people.

THIRD MOVEMENT

"Hornpipe"

A hornpipe is a lively and vigorous dance that is traditional among sailors. It appears in the third movement as a theme and variations.

Sea Rover Sonata

(See Analysis on page 30)

I First Movement

("Bell Bottom Trousers" and "Strike Up the Band, Here Comes a Sailor")

John W. Schaum

* **Note:** The clashing unharmonious sound (dissonance) of the G♮ and the G♯ in the bass is very effective when the music is played in tempo.

II Second Movement
(Rocked in the Cradle of the Deep)

III Third Movement
(Hornpipe)

＊Note: It doesn't matter exactly where the glissando begins or ends, as long as the left hand octave "D" receives a heavy accent.

Carnival in Poland

Ignace Jan Paderewski (pah-deh-REFF-skee), 1860-1941, was a famous Polish concert pianist, teacher, composer, and politician. He is best remembered for his piano compositions. In 1919 he held the office of Prime Minister of Poland. There is a monument to Paderewski in Washington, D.C. This piece is condensed from a piano solo titled, "Cracovienne" (see music dictionary on page 48).

Animato M.M. ♩ = 80

I. J. Paderewski, Op. 14, No. 6

Festivity

Henry K. Hadley (1871-1937) was an American composer who was educated at the New England Conservatory in Boston. He wrote symphonies, operas, chamber music, anthems, and piano music. In 1901 his Second Symphony won the Paderewski Prize. He is best remembered for his efforts to promote music of native American composers. This piece bears its original title.

Henry K. Hadley, Op. 14, No. 6

Note: When an italic *5* is placed over or under a group of five sixteenth notes, it signifies that they are to be played in the time of four sixteenth notes. The five notes are called **a quintuplet**.

Youthful rhythmic styles and modern harmonies: **GOSPEL PIANO PROFILES**

Rough and Ready

Paul Wachs (VAHX), 1851-1915, was a French composer, pianist, and organist educated at the Paris Conservatory where he was a student of Cesar Franck. He is best known for his piano compositions. This piece was originally titled "Capricante." (See music dictionary on page 48).

Paul Wachs

Making Music Quiz

DIRECTIONS: Match each musical term at the left with the correct definition at the right by inserting the corresponding alphabetical letter on the proper dotted line. For example, the answer to No. 1 is "gradually slower and louder", therefore the letter "c" has been placed on the dotted line.

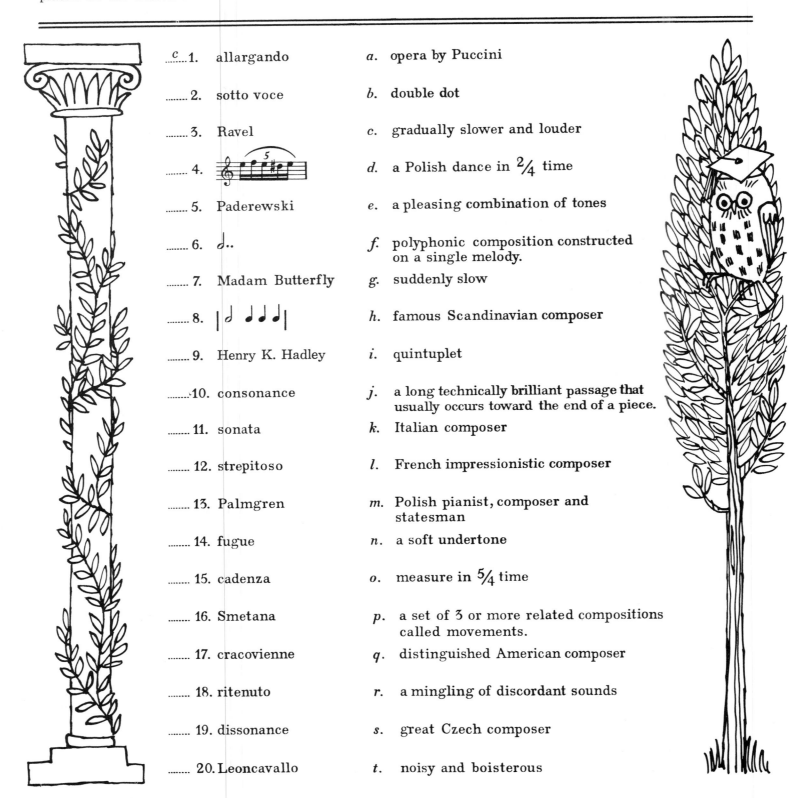

_c_ 1.	allargando	_a._	opera by Puccini
...... 2.	sotto voce	_b._	double dot
...... 3.	Ravel	_c._	gradually slower and louder
...... 4.		_d._	a Polish dance in 2/4 time
...... 5.	Paderewski	_e._	a pleasing combination of tones
...... 6.		_f._	polyphonic composition constructed on a single melody.
...... 7.	Madam Butterfly	_g._	suddenly slow
...... 8.		_h._	famous Scandinavian composer
...... 9.	Henry K. Hadley	_i._	quintuplet
...... 10.	consonance	_j._	a long technically brilliant passage that usually occurs toward the end of a piece.
...... 11.	sonata	_k._	Italian composer
...... 12.	strepitoso	_l._	French impressionistic composer
...... 13.	Palmgren	_m._	Polish pianist, composer and statesman
...... 14.	fugue	_n._	a soft undertone
...... 15.	cadenza	_o._	measure in 5/4 time
...... 16.	Smetana	_p._	a set of 3 or more related compositions called movements.
...... 17.	cracovienne	_q._	distinguished American composer
...... 18.	ritenuto	_r._	a mingling of discordant sounds
...... 19.	dissonance	_s._	great Czech composer
...... 20.	Leoncavallo	_t._	noisy and boisterous

Total Score ....

Certificate of Progress

This certifies that

_____

has successfully completed

the

JOHN W. SCHAUM

MAKING MUSIC

at the PIANO series

_____
TEACHER

_____
DATE

MUSIC DICTIONARY

Terms listed here are limited to those commonly found in Level Seven methods and supplements. However, many elementary terms such as *forte* and *piano* are not included because of limited space. The accented syllable is shown in *capital* letters. Tempo marks which consist of two or three words, such as *con brio*, or *meno mosso* are not listed here. It is intended that such terms be looked up one word at a time. This provides experience that will be valuable when working with a larger dictionary.

For a more complete listing, see the *Schaum Dictionary of Musical Terms*, a separate 1500-word compilation especially for keyboard students.

affettuoso (ah-fet-too-OH-soh) Affectionately.

agitato (ahd-jih-TAH-toh) Agitated; restless.

allargando (ah-lahr-GAHN-doh) Gradually slower and louder.

allegretto (ah-leh-GRET-toh) A little slower than *allegro*.

a tempo (ah TEHM-poh) Return to the previous tempo.

bravura (brah-VOO-rah) Boldness, brilliance. Music designed to display a performer's skills.

brillante (bree-LAHN-teh) Brilliant, showy.

brio (BREE-oh) Vigor, spirit, gusto.

cadenza (kah-DEN-zah) Elaborate ornamental musical passage exhibiting the skills of a solo performer.

cantabile (cahn-TAH-bil-lay) Singing style.

capricante (cah-pree-KAHN-tay) A musical creation in free form, whimsical in style.

capriccioso (cah-preet-chee-OH-soh) In a carefree or fanciful style.

chamber music Music involving a small group of performers for a small hall or parlor. Usually for various instrumental combinations from two to ten players. Most common is the quartet.

coda (KOH-dah) Extra musical section sometimes added at the end of a piece of music to emphasize the conclusion.

con (KONE) With.

consonance (CONN-suh-nunse) Combination of simultaneous musical sounds that are pleasing to the listener.

cracovienne (crack-oh-vee-ENN) Polish round dance in two-four time.

dissonance (DISS-uh-nunce) Combination of simultaneous musical sounds that are unpleasant or harsh to the listener. Often used to create dramatic effects: feelings of tension, unrest, or conflict which are usually resolved by a consonance.

dolce (DOL-chay) Sweetly, softly.

doloroso (doh-loh-ROH-soh) Sadly, sorrowfully.

eleganza (el-leh-GAHN-zah) Elegance, grace.

fz = **forzando** (fohr-TSAHN-doh) With force, energy.

giocoso (jee-oh-KOH-soh) Humorously, playfully.

glissando (glis-SUN-doh) Rapid gliding or sliding movement upward or downward. Produced by sliding a fingernail across white or black keys.

grandioso (grahn-dee-OH-soh) Dignified, majestic.

grazioso (gra-tsee-OH-soh) Gracefully.

humoresque (hu-mah-REHSK) Humorous or playful piece of music.

il basso (ill BAH-so) In the bass.

impressionism Style of music and art popular during the late 1800's and early 1900's especially in France. Purpose was to convey a mood, somewhat blurred vision, or general impression rather than specific details. Achieved by use of free-moving, colorful harmonies and tonalities plus unusual instrumental effects.

larghetto (lahr-GET-oh) Tempo a little faster than *largo*.

largo (LAHR-goh) Very slow, solemn.

legg. = **leggiero** (led-jee-AIR-oh) Light, delicate.

maestoso (my-ess-TOH-soh) Majestic, dignified; proudly.

marcato (mahr-CAH-toh) Marked, emphasized.

martellato (mahr-tel-LAH-toh) With heavy, hammer-like touch.

mattinata (mah-tin-NAH-tah) A morning melody.

meno (MAY-noh) Less.

molto (MOHL-toh) Very, much.

mosso (MOHS-soh) Moving, animated.

movement Main section or part of a larger work such as a symphony, sonata, or suite. Usually three or more movements (of contrasting style and tempo) are combined to form the larger work.

nocturne (NOK-turn) Title of music with a sentimental, romantic, or poetic character. (Literally: night piece.)

op. = **opus** (OH-pus) Musical work; may be a composition of any length from a short single piece to a full symphony. Usually numbered in chronological order.

opera (AH-per-ah) Secular musical drama with singing of vocal solos, ensembles, and choruses with orchestral accompaniment. Staged with a full array of costumes, props, scenery, lighting, special effects, etc.

pesante (peh-SAHN-teh) Heavy, weighty.

piu (PEE-oo) More.

poco (POH-koh) Little.

poco a poco (POH-koh ah POH-koh) Little by little, gradually.

rall. = **rallentando** (rah-lenn-TAHN-doh) Gradually growing slower.

ritenuto (ree-teh-NOO-toh) Slower, held back.

rococo (roh-KOH-koh) Style of music named after an extremely lavish and fancifully ornamented style of architecture popular during the 1700's.

rubato (roo-BAH-toh) Small slowings and accelerations of the tempo of a piece at the discretion of the performer or conductor to aid in expressing feelings and emotions.

scherzando (skare-TSAHN-doh) Playfully, jokingly.

semplice (SEMM-plee-chay) Simple, plain.

sonatine (sonn-ah-TEEN) Sonatina; a short sonata, usually less difficult and with a simpler form. Generally has fewer themes, shorter development, and fewer movements than a sonata.

sotto voce (SOH-toh VOH-chay) Subdued or reduced in sound.

strepitoso (streh-pee-TOH-soh) Noisy, furious.

suite (SWEET) 1) Piece of instrumental music made up of several sections or movements, usually in varying style and tempo. 2) Group of excerpts from a larger musical work such as a ballet or musical show. The "Nutcracker Suite" is the most famous example.

symphony (SYM-foh-nee) Large piece of music written for orchestra in sonata form. Although it is usual to have four movements, the number of movements, along with the instrumentation and style vary with each composer and the time it was written.

ten. = **tenuto** (teh-NOO-toh) Sustained; held to full value.

theme and variations Type of musical form in which one theme has many repetitions, each time with various changes of style or accompaniment.

tranquillo (trahn-KWILL-oh) Tranquil, quiet.

vigoroso (vig-oh-ROH-soh) Vigorous, forceful, energetic.

vivace (vee-VAH-chay) Lively, quick.